Electa M Bronson Sheldon

The Clevelands

Showing the Influence of a Christian Family in a New Settlement

Electa M Bronson Sheldon

The Clevelands
Showing the Influence of a Christian Family in a New Settlement

ISBN/EAN: 9783337027810

Printed in Europe, USA, Canada, Australia, Japan

Cover: Foto ©ninafisch / pixelio.de

More available books at **www.hansebooks.com**

THE CLEVELANDS:

SHOWING THE

INFLUENCE OF A CHRISTIAN FAMILY

IN A NEW SETTLEMENT.

BY

MRS. E. M. SHELDON.

> Where once was heard the savage yell
> Ascends the Christian's prayer,
> And sweetly sounds the Sabbath bell
> Along the morning air.
> On Nature's charms how calmly smiles
> That hallowed morn in western wilds!

PUBLISHED BY THE
AMERICAN TRACT SOCIETY,
28 CORNHILL, BOSTON.

PREFACE.

No element is more important to the growth and prosperity of a young village, in a newly-settled country, than religion. By many this is sadly forgotten, and many, who in their former homes had borne the Christian name, neglect, on removing into the wilderness, to carry their profession and piety with them.

The narrative which follows (which the Authoress assures us is substantially true, except as to names, &c.) is that of a family who begun life in their new home as Christians. It illustrates how much may be accomplished by such a family, in an unostentatious way, for the promotion of religion around them, and in planting the germs of Christian institutions in our rising communities. It is earnestly commended to the imitation of all those similarly situated, whether at the East or the West.

EDITOR.

CONTENTS.

CHAPTER I.
                                                        PAGE
THE ARRIVAL. 5

CHAPTER II.
REASONS FOR REMOVAL. 11

CHAPTER III.
PLANS. 20

CHAPTER IV.
FIRST SABBATH IN THE WILDERNESS. 24

CHAPTER V.
NEIGHBORLY CALLS. 35

CHAPTER VI.

THE CHILDREN'S PARTY................ 43

CHAPTER VII.

SHALL WE HAVE A SABBATH SCHOOL?......... 56

CHAPTER VIII.

THE SABBATH SCHOOL BEGUN.............. 71

CHAPTER IX.

THE PRAYER MEETING................ 78

CHAPTER X.

FRUITS........................ 85

THE CLEVELANDS.

CHAPTER I.

THE ARRIVAL.

The ax rang sharply 'mid those forest shades
Which from creation toward the sky had towered,
In unshorn beauty. There, with vigorous arm,
Wrought the bold emigrant, and by his side
His little son, with question and response,
Beguiled the time.
MRS. SIGOURNEY'S POEMS.

AT the close of a lovely day in May, 18—, three heavily-loaded, covered wagons, drawn by sturdy oxen, emerged from one of the dense forests, then so common in Michigan, into an opening made by the first settlers of the village of Smithton. The poor cattle panted with fatigue, as they dragged along their loads of "goods and chattels;" and the living occupants of the last wagon of the trio were silent and thoughtful.

"Stop a moment, Mike, and let the oxen breathe," shouted Mr. Cleveland, the driver of the last team, to the one in advance. "George, my son," continued he, as they halted, addressing a noble-looking lad, about fourteen years of age, who drove the second team, "you look very tired: the road is smooth the rest of the way; so jump on the wagon, and let *your* oxen take care of themselves; they will follow the team ahead well enough."

"Not very tired, father; it is not far now, and I would rather walk, if you please," said George, who was not a little proud of the dexterity with which he could guide his "horned horses," as he termed them.

"Papa, papa! where is that famous village?" said a sprightly little girl of nine. "I have looked, and looked, till my eyes ache, and have finally concluded it must belong to fairies, who have wickedly hid it from poor, tired mortals like us."

"A sage conclusion, truly," replied her father, smiling; "especially when that same village, as Mike says, is right before you."

"Why, papa," exclaimed the astonished

child, "you don't call those four or five log huts a village — do you?"

"Certainly I do, my dear little Ella. That is a Michigan village. How do you like it?"

"Oh Mary! do look! What a splendid place! What a large village!" said Ella to the pensive sister, two years older than herself, who sat by her side; and the merry little girl clapped her hands with glee, while her light, ringing laugh was sweet music to her father's ear, whose heart ached when he thought of the many privations to which his loved ones must be subjected in their western home.

"Now I must count the houses as we pass through," continued the little chatterbox; "so please, Miss Sobriety, don't interrupt me."

"Dear mamma," half whispered Mary, "how different all this is from the scenery around our old home — that so cheerful, this so silent and lonely. Don't you think we shall all be homesick?"

"We shall, undoubtedly, have many trials,

my daughter," replied her mother; "but you know the divine promise, '*My grace is sufficient for thee.*' But cheer up, my dear, don't let papa see you sad; we will talk more of this another time."

"One, two, three private dwelling houses, one tavern, and ———. Mamma, what is that little, low building, opposite the tavern?" asked Ella, as they drove slowly through the village.

"That, my dear, is a blacksmith's shop. Those horseshoe prints, burned on the door, are his sign."

"Do see the heads at the doors and windows," said Ella, lowering her voice almost to a whisper. "I do believe every inhabitant of this extensive village is gazing at us; but I don't think it very good manners to stare so."

"Oh, how beautiful! How beautiful!" suddenly exclaimed Mary, as the sun, which had been for some time obscured by a cloud, burst forth in the full splendor of his setting rays. "Just look, mamma, Ella, and Kate— see how the tall trees, with their tender leaves, the rough houses, and even the stumps and the ground, are deluged in a sea of glory!

> 'These are thy works, almighty Father — these
> Are but the varied God,'"

said the young enthusiast, reverently clasping her hands, and raising her eyes to heaven. "If," murmured she, as if thinking aloud,— "if Michigan has many such scenes as this, I shall not be homesick. 'Twill be impossible."

Her mother gazed tearfully upon her during this burst of feeling; but the thoughts and attention of all were soon diverted into a new channel by their arrival at their long-wished-for home.

"Where are we, mamma?" said little Frank, who had been asleep for some time on a bed in the wagon, and was now aroused by the noisy glee of Ella.

"We are at our new home, my little boy," said his father, who had just helped the girls from their rather high seat to terra firma, and now set out little Frank; then, turning to his wife, he whispered, as he assisted her to alight, " Welcome to your new home, dearest. Poor though it be, it is the best that even your husband's love can provide."

" We shall be happy, very happy here, dear Edward, if *you* do not despond. Cheer up, my husband; mutual affection will make this wild spot a paradise."

By the time the older members of the family were ready to enter, Ella,—who was always foremost,— George, Frank, and even Mary,—who, in the novelty and excitement, had lost all thoughts of home-sickness,—had ransacked the house, which was built of logs, and not very spacious, and now stood at the door, with mock gravity, to give their parents, and Mike, and Kate, a gracious welcome.

CHAPTER II.

REASONS FOR REMOVAL.

*The good are better made by ill,
As odors crushed are sweeter still.*
                    ROGERS' JACQUELINE.

EDWARD CLEVELAND and Julia Westbury were born, educated, and married in the city of Boston. Their parents were wealthy; but, unlike too many wealthy families, they felt that an abundance of this world's goods was no excuse for neglecting the moral culture of their children. Acquainted from childhood, the union of Edward and Julia seemed more the natural result of similar tastes, habits, and modes of thinking, than the consummation of a romantic attachment. Soon after their marriage they removed to New York, where Mr. Cleveland's father established him in a flourishing business. And now, amid the engrossing cares and alluring temptations of mercantile life, how often did he thank Heaven for those active business habits and the stern integrity that had been his daily lessons from boyhood!

Years passed away, and the tide of their united life, like the tide of their early love, did run smooth. Four happy, blooming children were as olive plants around their table. Wealth rolled in upon them, and Mrs. Cleveland, as the affectionate wife, the fond and pious mother, amply sustained the fair promise of her girlhood. Nothing of earth could add to the happiness of this interesting family which was not already enjoyed. But a reverse came. Amid the commercial crash that hurled thousands from affluence to abject poverty, Mr. Cleveland found his affairs so embarrassed by the failure of many indebted to him, that his own fair inheritance must be scattered to the winds. None but those who have passed through the same fiery ordeal can realize his distress of mind, when the painful truth first burst upon his bewildered senses. For days, he and his confidential clerk had been busily engaged in a thorough investigation of their complicated business matters; and when, at last, every thing was adjusted, and but a few hundreds remained, after all liabilities should be paid, is it wonderful that the strong man bowed his head, and became a very child again?

"Excuse this weakness, Morton," said Mr. Cleveland, as, with a powerful effort, he regained his usual composure. "You have been a faithful, tried friend for years; would that I could reward you; but that now is impossible. However, thanks to a merciful Providence, there is enough left to pay all my debts; so you will not lose your hard-earned wages, nor will any widow or orphans curse me for their distress. Stay with me, Morton," continued he, "till my affairs are settled, and my gratitude shall be for ever yours."

"Mr. Cleveland," replied the young man, "I have received many favors from you; and, were it not for my mother and sisters, what little is due for my services I would never receive; but, for their sakes, my hand must accept what my heart refuses. Command me in all things through your coming trial, and I shall be but too happy to serve you. Hark! the bells strike twelve o'clock! Will not your wife be alarmed at your unusual absence?"

"Poor Julia! how will she bear it?" murmured Mr. Cleveland.

"Your wife is a woman and a Christian, sir," said Morton, as he bade his employer good night.

"A woman and a Christian," repeated the poor husband, as he walked slowly homeward. "Yes, so she is, and a true one, too; but she has never been poor; she has never known want; it will kill her; she can not bear it; and my poor children, too, what will become of them?"

Mr. Cleveland had reached home, and mechanically mounted the steps; but, as he placed his hand upon the knob, his courage forsook him, and he leaned against the house for support. It was but for a moment. The quick ear of his watchful wife had long since learned, that

"His very foot had music in't,
When he came up the stairs;"

and she now hastened to him, and, though greatly alarmed, drew him gently into the parlor.

"Edward! dear husband!" exclaimed she, as she gazed on his pale, haggard face, "what is the matter? What has happened? Are you ill?"

"Sick? Yes, sick at heart!" said he, with a nervous start. "Julia, we are ruined."

"Tell me, Edward, is that all? Is that the worst intelligence you bring?"

"Is not that enough?" exclaimed he, petulantly.

"Edward Cleveland," replied his wife, in a half-reproving tone, "you profess to be a Christian. Shall we receive good at the hand of the Lord, and not evil? Compose yourself," she added, tenderly, "and let us talk over the matter calmly. I will be with you again presently;" and, taking a light, she withdrew to the kitchen, to which, though amply supplied with domestics, she was by no means a stranger. Here she busied herself for some time in preparing some slight refreshments for him, whose physical powers were fast giving way under the intense mental excitement to which they had been so long subjected, and which he had made such efforts to conceal from his family.

Mr. Cleveland paced the room in great agitation for some minutes after his wife left; but her words of encouragement, her calmness, and the expression of relief in her countenance, when he told her the news, — which he thought would quite overcome her, — quieted his fears, and imparted to his mind a tranquillity which an hour before he would have deemed it impossible ever again to possess. When Mrs. Cleveland returned, after an absence purposely protracted, she found her husband composed, willing to converse on the painful subject of their present embarrassments, and gathering new strength for future action, as he unbosomed himself to her who had so long enjoyed his confidence.

"Why, Julia! you are quite a cook; for I suppose Kate went to bed long ago," said Mr. Cleveland, as his wife pushed back the table, after their midnight repast.

"Has my husband yet to learn," replied she, "that my excellent mother instructed me not only in the superintendence, but in all the minutiæ, of domestic affairs?"

"That will make poverty rather easier to bear," half whispered her husband, with a sigh.

"Hush, hush," said Mrs. Cleveland, playfully; "*you* may be as poor as you please; but while my husband and children are spared me, *I* shall be rich."

In a few weeks Mr. Cleveland had settled up his business, disposed of his costly house and furniture, dismissed his clerks and domestics, removed his family to a small but comfortable cottage, just out of the city, which he had formerly rented, and was upon the eve of his departure for that El Dorado of the unfortunate—the "West."

"Well, Mike," said he to an Irishman, who had been his porter, but who, for the last few weeks, had served him as man of all work, "you know I start for Michigan tomorrow; and what can I do for you before I go? The Stuarts want a porter; would you like a recommendation?"

"And sure, Mr. Cleveland," replied Mike, "it's not sending me away you're going to?"

"I would like very much to keep you, Mike, but you know I am poor now, and can not pay you the wages I have done hitherto. So I see no other way than for you to find a more prosperous employer."

"And Kate?"

"Mrs. Cleveland thinks she must do her own housework; but the elder Stuart wants a housekeeper; so you and Kate won't be separated. Are you satisfied, my good fellow?" asked Mr. Cleveland, smiling.

Mike shrugged his shoulders, hesitated a moment, and then said, "Kate and I were talking over that same going west last night; and we thought we would like to go too. So, if you will buy us a lot of land close by your own, and give us our board, we will stay with you and serve you faithfully till this fall a year. And then," said he, "we will get married, and set up housekeeping ourselves."

"But that will be making too great a sacrifice," returned Mr. Cleveland; "you must look out for your own interest better than this, or you will never do to get married."

"You was kind to me, sir, when I was a stranger in America," said the honest fellow, brushing away a tear, "and I don't like the leaving of you now, unless Kate and I would be a burden."

"Many thanks for your affectionate regard," said Mr. Cleveland, with emotion: "stay with us; and if we prosper, you shall not be forgotten."

We will pass over the tender parting of Mr. Cleveland with his loving and beloved family; the loneliness of his journey, which was not then, as now, that of a day; the difficulty of selecting a location where all the country was so beautiful; the building of his future residence; his safe return; the dull monotony of the ensuing winter, and the perplexities and perils of their immigration, and return to our rather verdant "Wolverines."

CHAPTER III.

PLANS.

*When the purposes of life
Stood apart from vulgar strife,
Labor in the path of duty
Gleamed up like a thing of beauty.*
                                          C. P. CRANCH.

It was Monday when our immigrants reached Smithton, having spent the Sabbath at A——, one of the oldest and most flourishing villages in the state; and the next Saturday evening found them quite comfortably settled in their "log mansion," as Ella called it. Mr. Cleveland, George, and Mike had gone to look for the cattle, whose pasture was abundant and very extensive, unobstructed by fences or bars. Kate was clearing away the tea things; and the girls and little Frank had drawn their stools close around their mother, who sat at the open window, busy with her needle.

"Mamma," said Mary, "can you tell us, now, what are your plans for us in the future? You told us yesterday that we must adopt a regular system; and can't we begin next week?"

"Heigh-ho! I hope mamma will not install me dish-washer," said Ella. "I don't like the trade at all."

"I hope my daughters will think their mother knows best what will make them most useful and happy hereafter, and be willing to do as she thinks proper, even if the task be not quite so pleasant."

"Oh, yes, mamma," exclaimed both the girls at once. "But now for those plans, if you please," said Ella.

"Well, then, first,—and probably most unpleasant of all,—Mary and you must clear the table and wash the dishes after breakfast and dinner, every day, when you are in health. You will pursue the same course, before breakfast, that you have pursued for a few months past. You will all spend an hour or two every forenoon and afternoon at your lessons; and after tea we will spend the time in music, walking, &c."

"Will George and I have to study, too?" said Frank.

"Certainly, my son," replied his mother; "we live in the woods, now, where there are no schools suitable for George; and you, Frank, are getting old enough to learn something beside play."

"Oh, I know a great many things now," said Frank. "I thought it would always be holiday here in the woods," added he, musingly.

"I did not suppose my little boy would want to grow up a dunce, coarse, vulgar, and uneducated, if he does live in the woods," replied Mrs. Cleveland; "but, Frank, you need not study, unless you choose."

"I *will* study, mamma; for I want to know as much as any body."

"It is Saturday night," said Mary; "how shall we spend the Sabbath? Do they have Sabbath schools and meetings here?"

"They have occasional preaching at the village," replied her mother; "but there is no Sabbath school; and, as there is but one pious family in Smithton, there are no prayer meetings. There is no preaching to-morrow; so we must spend the day at home; and I hope it will not be entirely unprofitable."

"Mamma, if there is no Sabbath school, we shall not have to learn a verse a day, in addition to our morning reading; shall we?" said Ella.

"Yes;" replied Mrs. Cleveland, "for we shall have a Sabbath school at home."

"But if there is one pious family to help us, why can't we have a Sabbath school at the village?" asked Mary.

"Perhaps we may, when the people become well acquainted with us; but the habits of those who have been brought up in the country are very different from those of city people, and we must be careful not to become prejudiced against each other. Here comes Mike with the cows; so we must not talk any more now."

CHAPTER IV.

FIRST SABBATH IN THE WILDERNESS.

All nature rests ; the flocks and herds, listless
And silent, crop the needed fruit, then seek
Repose, or gather 'neath the shady oak,
As if they knew to-day were holy time.

The Sabbath dawned as bright and lovely on the forest home of the Clevelands, as when its blessed light dispelled the darkness from their city habitation; and to the enthusiastic minds of the children it seemed more beautiful. The matin song of the birds seemed sweeter and holier than usual. The cattle moved quietly away to graze, and soft zephyrs whispered to the green leaves, " 'Tis holy time."

The morning was pleasantly spent by Mr. and Mrs. Cleveland in reading the Scriptures, and conversing with their children and domestics on the important truths and striking historical events, which can not fail, if judiciously presented to the mind, both to entertain and instruct. In the afternoon, the family formed themselves into a Bible class, with Mr. Cleveland for teacher; the children reciting their lessons learned on the verse-a-day system; then all, with open Bibles, answering in turn the questions that presented themselves to their teacher's mind. Mr. and Mrs. Cleveland were alike united in their views of family government and religion. Their religion was not a Sabbath day's garb of holiness, but a fixed principle, an all-pervading sentiment, entering into and incorporated with their whole life. Deeming the Sabbath a temporal as well as a spiritual blessing, they strove to make it a delight to their household, and they, thus far, had been eminently successful. Never had they heard their young children complain of weariness, or exclaim, "When will the Sabbath be past?" and now, when they were entering almost upon a new existence, they were anxious to pursue such a course that holy time, even deprived, as they were, of the privileges of the sanctuary, should be hailed as an inestimable blessing — a day of privileged enjoyment, not as one of irksome task work.

Toward evening of this their first Sabbath in the wilderness, the family were listening to the latest missionary intelligence, read by Mr. Cleveland, when the attention of little Frank, who sat near the window, was attracted by three men, who came sauntering up the road from the village. Their appearance was any thing but prepossessing. To be sure, their week-old beards had undergone a pretended process of shaving, and their coarse linen was clean; but their outer garments bore evident marks of long service; and here a rip and there a rent showed the want of woman's tidy hand; and there was a certain care-for-nothing air about them, which would very readily place them with the class denominated loafers. They continued to advance slowly towards the house, till they reached the rude fence that enclosed Mr. Cleveland's little clearing. Here they stopped, and seemed consulting together whether they should advance to the house or return.

Just then Mr. Cleveland raised his eyes, and, stepping to the door, invited them in.

"Thank'ee, sir," said Mr. Smith, the tavern keeper; "we were walking out to take the air, and thought it would be no more than friendly just to give you a call. This is neighbor Johnson, Mr. Cleveland; and this is my son John," continued he, awkwardly, pointing to the individuals as he spoke.

"Be seated, gentlemen," said Mr. Cleveland, after acknowledging the uncouth introduction.

"You were reading when we came in; perhaps we interrupted you," said Mr. Johnson.

"Yes, I was reading some missionary news to my family, and if you would like to hear it, I will continue," was the reply.

"Thank'ee, sir," said they all.

After finishing the article he had commenced, and reading one or two other short pieces, that he thought would be likely to interest them, Mr. Cleveland paused, made a few remarks on the importance and success of missionary labor, then, turning to his visitors, asked them some questions with regard to their own religious privileges.

"I have been told," said he, "that you have preaching here occasionally. May I ask how often?"

"Yes," said Mr. Smith, "there is a Methodist preacher, who comes and preaches once in four weeks, at the school house in the village. They say he preaches very well, but I never heard him. I think I shall go next time he comes."

"When will he preach again?" asked Mrs. Cleveland.

"Next Sunday, at eleven o'clock, ma'am. I s'pose you and the children will come; won't you?"

"Oh, yes, if we are well. But where is the school house? We did not notice it when we came through."

"You can't see it from the road you came on, ma'am," replied Mr. Smith. "It stands behind a clump of trees, on the road that runs north of my house. Now, while I think of it, my wife said this morning, that she meant to come out and see you this week."

"I hope she will," replied Mrs. Cleveland. "I have not had the pleasure of seeing any of my neighbors yet."

The men now rose to go; and, after bidding Mrs. Cleveland good evening, they asked Mr. Cleveland to accompany them home, "just to stir his blood," as they said.

"Thank you. Not to-day; it is the Sabbath; but I shall be at the village to-morrow, and will see you then."

"Cleveland seems to be a clever fellow, but I am sorry he is so dreadful religious," said Smith, as soon as they were out of hearing. "Now there's Brown, you know, won't never drink a drop, make a bet, nor do any thing that has a bit of fun in it, just because of this plaguy religion. I was in hopes we shouldn't have any more pious folks in Smithton."

"I don't know what to think of this religion," replied Johnson. "When I was a little child, my mother used to make me say my prayers every night, and in the morning she used to read and pray, for my father was dead, and though she had to work hard to support her children, she always seemed happy. Brown seems to be happy; and Brown gets along well, too; better than I do, though he was poor when he came here; and I had a good farm then, with almost as much improvement as I have now. Cleveland's family look happier than mine; and I almost believe it is owing to their religion."

"Father," said John, "did you notice he said he could not go with us because it was Sunday? Pretty good hint for us to stay away; wasn't it?"

"Yes, I thought so; didn't you, neighbor Johnson?"

"Yes; but like enough he didn't mean it as a hint," was the reply.

By this time they had reached the village, and the trio separated — Johnson to call up long-buried memories of his pious mother and his early childhood, during his solitary walk home, and Smith and his son to relate all they had seen and heard at the Clevelands to the little knot of loungers at the tavern.

George Cleveland sat gazing abstractedly after the retreating visitors, till an angle in the road hid them from view. Starting like one waking from a troubled dream, he turned to his father, half opened his lips as if to speak, then, hesitating, cast his eyes to the floor.

"Speak out," said his father, with a smile, who conjectured what was passing in his mind; "you need not fear to place confidence in your parents."

"I am not afraid, father; but I did not know but it would be disrespectful to tell you what I was thinking of."

"My children are not often disrespectful; so I shall not be very suspicious. But what were you going to say, George?"

"I was thinking, if we had been in New York when those men called, you would not have invited them in; and I could not understand why you should do any differently here."

"Professing Christians," said Mr. Cleveland, "should always endeavor to be consistent. Different circumstances may induce them to pursue a course which will seem entirely inconsistent with their previous course of conduct and their avowed principles, when, if their motives were known, all appearance of inconsistency would vanish. There is not a vagrant in the streets of New York who is not sufficiently well informed to know how Christians regard the Sabbath; and a call from them, or from any of our acquaintance, merely as a matter of ceremony or friendship, would justly be considered as an insult, and deserve to be received as such; but here, my children, in this western wilderness, the case is different; the outward restraints of religion do not exist; there are but few meetings, and no Sabbath schools — but little to remind one that a seventh part of the time is Jehovah's. These men have been brought up in a land of Sabbaths, as well as ourselves, but to them Sunday was a day of restraint and weariness, and when they came to the west they threw off that restraint; and now they almost seem to have forgotten why the Sabbath is observed."

"Do they work on Sunday, papa?" said Frank.

"No, they do not work unless in what they think a case of necessity, as in securing their hay or wheat crops; but they visit, hunt, fish, and congregate at the tavern, which is far more destructive to the morals than mere manual labor. Yet beneath a rough exterior and unpolished manners may be concealed virtues that would do honor to the most refined and proudest of our countrymen; beside, it will teach us humility, forbearance, and gratitude — three lessons that can not be too well studied by poor wayward mortals like ourselves."

"Papa, one question more," said George, "if you please. Is it wrong to walk out on the Sabbath?"

"That will depend on the motives we have in walking, where we walk, and the influence we shall exert upon others. If we walk within the bounds of our own inclosure, for exercise, there can not any harm arise, as I can see, to ourselves or others, by so doing; nor would there be any thing wrong, as far as ourselves are concerned, in wandering out into the forest among nature's beauties, if we were thus led to look from nature up to nature's God. But suppose, in one of these rambles, we should chance to meet a hunter, an habitual Sabbath breaker; would he not think himself almost justified in his course, if he could say, in answer to reproof, 'Why, Mr. Such-a-one, a very good man, walks out on Sunday, for I met him a week or two ago in the woods, as much as a mile from his house'? So, you see, an act may be innocent in itself, and yet hurtful in its influence upon others. Had I gone to the village with those men to-day, though I had talked all the way on religious subjects, my influence with them would have been for ever gone. The fact that I walked out with them on the Sabbath would have been to them a shield against reproof, whatever were my motives in going. And now, my children, you will doubtless see many things in your mother's course of life and my own that you may not understand. We are placed in entirely different circumstances from those of former years, and when any such incidents occur, wait till a proper time, then come and ask us unreservedly the reasons why, as you have done to-day; and may a kind Father give us grace so to live, that it will always be a pleasure to us to explain our motives to our children."

CHAPTER V.

NEIGHBORLY CALLS.

We pine for kindred natures
To mingle with our own
MRS. HEMANS.

"Good morning, Mrs. Brown," said Mrs. Smith, the tavern-keeper's wife, as she unceremoniously entered the house of the worthy blacksmith, early the following Tuesday.

"Good morning," was the reply of Mrs. Brown, who was busy about her household affairs. "Won't you take a seat, Mrs. Smith? You must have risen earlier than we did, to have your work out of the way so soon."

"Oh, bless you, no. We haven't been up over half an hour; and, to tell you the truth, we hain't been to breakfast yet — but I can't stop to sit. I come to ask you if you wouldn't like to go up to Cleveland's a-visiting this afternoon."

"Yes, I would like to become acquainted with our new neighbors. I was thinking yesterday whether they had been here long enough to get settled, so as to like to see company."

"Settled!" repeated Mrs. Smith; "why, my husband was in there on Sunday, and he said every thing was as neat as a pin, and they looked as if they had lived there a year. He told them I was coming up this week. Well, I must be going. You will be ready early; won't you?"

"As soon as I can after dinner," was the reply.

"So Smith called on the Clevelands on

Sunday! I wonder how he was received, for they say they are pious," thought Mrs. Brown, after her neighbor left. "Oh, I wish I could find a companion and friend in Mrs. Cleveland; I have been here so long shut out from the society of those who could enter into my feelings, that I earnestly desire one female friend to whom I can pour out my full soul. But Mrs. Cleveland is better educated, and her tastes and talents are more cultivated, than mine; however, if our minds are similarly constituted, her superior advantages ought not to make any difference."

The Brown family was vastly superior in mental and moral worth to the other inhabitants of the village. They had never been wealthy, nor had the parents, when young, enjoyed any other advantages for education than those afforded by attending the district school a few months in a year; but they, like the truly wise, sought the pearl of great price early in youth, and were thus kept from vice, and brought to seek permanent earthly happiness in their own mental culture, and in training their children in wisdom's ways, which are indeed ways of pleasantness.

During their walk to Mr. Cleveland's, Mrs. Brown heard from her talkative companion all the particulars of the Sunday visit; and on their arrival, she found her flurried spirits suddenly reassured by the kind reception of Mrs. Cleveland. In the course of the afternoon, Mrs. Brown learned that Mrs. Cleveland educated her own children, and that they had just resumed their studies since their arrival, and the desire arose in her mind that her only daughter might be under the care of such an instructress.

"But you do not expect to complete the education of your children, I suppose," said she to Mrs. Cleveland.

"If I live and am blessed with health, I hope to complete that of our daughters," she replied. "Our sons we wish to send to college. George is now fourteen, and has nearly finished his preparatory course. His bachelor uncle, whose name he bears, has kindly offered to defray his expenses through his collegiate course; and we hope to send him east next fall, or in the spring, at the furthest. Frank, our youngest, is but a little boy yet, and will for years be under my care, if his life is spared."

"La, me," said Mrs. Smith, "I shouldn't think of teaching my children at home. I couldn't never have patience. We calculate, when we get a little richer, to send our two oldest girls away to school. As for John, who was here on Sunday, he says he knows enough without any more book learnin'. He can read, write, and cipher, and that is enough. As for the younger children, we shall most likely be rich enough to let them go to school or not, as they are a mind to. We mean to have them learn to read and write, at any rate — they can learn that at the district school."

Here Kate's summons to tea interrupted the conversation, and the visitors soon after took their leave.

"How perfectly disgusting Mrs. Smith is in her boast of wealth, proprietorship of the village, farms, &c.," said Mrs. Brown to her husband that evening, when they found themselves alone. "Mrs. Cleveland is too intelligent not to read the character of Mrs.

Smith at once; otherwise, she must have considered some of her conversation this afternoon really insulting."

"Mrs. Smith is certainly a weak-minded woman," replied Mr. Brown; "but how do you like Mrs. Cleveland?"

"She appears like a lovely woman. I often thought this afternoon that she might prove just the friend I have so long wished for, if she should consider me worthy of her friendship."

"Worthy of her friendship! If she is worthy of yours, she will not consider you inferior to herself. Believe me, dear wife, this lack of self-esteem causes you many unhappy moments. A virtuous, right-minded woman, one who tries to perform well the duties of a friend, a wife, and a mother, is not beneath any of the sex in the scale of worth, whatever may be her station in life — nor will the truly great, good, and lovely, of either sex, consider her so."

Tears were in the eyes of Mrs. Brown, as she replied, "I acknowledge the truth of all you have said; but I can not overcome that weakness in my character. Perhaps," she added, with a faint smile, "you will think me too presuming when I tell you another thought I had. Mrs. Cleveland educates her own children, and I could not help wishing that Clara might be under her care and instruction."

"It would indeed be very desirable," said Mr. Brown, "and when you become more acquainted with Mrs. Cleveland, you can tell how she would receive a proposition to that effect."

In a few weeks Mrs. Cleveland had received visits from most of her neighbors, and commenced returning them, taking care to visit in the same rotation that she had received their attentions, that there might be no reason to accuse her of slight or preference. Mrs. Smith and Mrs. Brown she visited on two succeeding days, the former lady first, as she considered her most likely to take offense. On her return from Mrs. Brown's, she told her little girls she had an invitation for them to visit Mrs. Smith on the following day.

"She has invited quite a party of little girls to meet you, and I hope you will remember to treat them politely. And now," continued Mrs. Cleveland, "I have something of more importance than our visit to communicate. I have promised Mrs. Brown to receive her little Clara into our family school."

"O, we shall be so happy to have a playmate!" said the delighted Ella, clapping her hands. "How old is she, mamma?"

"She is about Mary's age, but will class with you, Ella. You will see her to-morrow at Mrs. Smith's; but be careful not to show her any preference, nor even mention this arrangement, unless some one else speaks of it first. Now, my daughters, good night; for mamma is overtired."

CHAPTER VI.

THE CHILDREN'S PARTY.

> Disgust concealed
> Is ofttimes proof of wisdom, when the fault
> Is obstinate, and cure beyond our reach.
> COWPER'S TASK.

"Home again, and I am glad of it!" exclaimed Ella Cleveland, petulantly, as she ran into the house the following evening, and, throwing her bonnet on the table, flung herself into a chair. Mary followed, with a frown on her brow, but she was more quiet in her indignation.

"Why, girls, what has happened to disturb you so?" said their mother, looking up from her sewing.

"I never want to visit any more country girls as long as I live," said Ella, tossing her head. "I never saw such an ill-mannered set in my life. They have done nothing but insult us the whole afternoon."

"Who were they, and what did they do?" asked Mrs. Cleveland, quietly.

"There was a daughter of Mr. Johnson, who made us the call on Sunday, two daughters of Mr. Jones, who lives in the village, Clara Brown, Mr. Smith's two girls, and ourselves. The rest were all there when we came. Mrs. Smith told us to take off our bonnets and make ourselves at home, and we were left to find out the names of our new mates as we could. All the girls had knitting work, and they were just then very industrious. No one spoke to us, but they whispered among themselves about city girls, idleness — felt above work, &c. Finally Mrs. Smith came in, and seeing Mary and me look rather sad, I suppose, she proposed that we should walk out to see the village. The girls paired off, leaving Mary and me by ourselves; but Clara Brown whispered to Lizzie Johnson, and they came and offered to walk with us. We found them very pleasant girls, and were for a little while quite happy. After we had walked about a while, the Smith girls proposed that we should visit the school house. When we got into the grove on this side, the girls whispered together; and then, as we passed one tree after another, they asked us what sort of wood they were, saying we had so much learning we must certainly know. When we told them we did not know, they laughed as loud as they could, and said all that book learning was good for was to make folks lazy, and feel above their neighbors. We did not say any thing; but when the Jones and Smith girls had gone into the school house, we could not keep from crying. Clara and Lizzie had not laughed with the rest, and when they saw how bad we felt, they tried all they could to comfort us. Clara said such treatment was not right, and she went to the door of the school house to talk to the girls. In a moment she came running back as pale as death. 'O girls,' said she, ' don't you think they have got a mock meeting there; come and see for yourselves.' So we all went to the door, and sure enough there they were all kneeling, and one of them praying in a tone of perfect mockery. Pretty soon they got up, and one of the girls went behind the teacher's desk, and said she was going to preach. They asked us to come in and take seats, but we were too much shocked with their impiety; so we went back to Mr. Smith's as fast as we could. When we reached the house, we found tea ready, and the other girls coming soon, we took tea, and were very glad you told us to return early; so we started for home. Clara whispered, as she bade us 'Good by,' that she should commence her lessons next week, and Lizzie said she should come and see us very soon. The other girls said they would come a piece with us. We begged them not to trouble themselves; but come they would, and as it was nearer, we took a path across the fields. We soon learned the object of their seeming kindness; they would ask about the different kinds of grain that we saw growing, and when we confessed our ignorance of all kinds except corn, they would laugh and whisper among themselves. The last field we passed through was thickly covered with a low plant, bearing very small blue flowers. One of the girls asked Mary if she ever saw any flax growing. Mary answered, 'No.' 'Well,' said she, 'this is flax.' 'I think not,' replied sister; 'it grows too near the ground.' 'That is because it is young,' was the reply. But no sooner had Mary broken off some of the plant to examine it, than they all burst into a loud, coarse laugh, called us 'little fools,' and ran for home.

"We were glad to escape from our tormentors, and did not stop till we found ourselves in our own yard. Now, mamma," continued Ella, "this is a long story, and a strange one, too; but ask Mary if it is not strictly true."

"True! yes, indeed; only Ella could not tell all the significant looks, the winks, and sly whisperings, which are so annoying. Now, mamma, after being so treated, don't you think it best for us to drop all intercourse with those ill-mannered girls?"

"You have not been very politely treated, it is true, and I do not want you to be intimate with them; but I think an occasional interchange of visits may be rather beneficial to you than otherwise."

"Why, mamma, how can it be beneficial to us? For you early taught us that evil communications corrupt good manners; that a person is known by the company he keeps; how, then, can we be benefited by such associates?"

"Perhaps an explanation of my reasons would not be very agreeable, if it involved telling my daughters their faults," said Mrs. Cleveland, smiling.

"We must try to correct our faults, if 'tis not quite so pleasant; so please explain, mamma," said Mary, after musing a while.

"We were created social beings," said Mrs. Cleveland, "and at the same time an all-wise Creator has given to his creatures different tastes, modes of thinking, and traits of character; some, if we may so speak, are naturally amiable and virtuous; others seem to delight in nothing so much as vice and mischief: education and example either strengthen or change the natural bent of the character. These very girls that have treated you so ill have undoubtedly some virtues; indeed, their bad conduct may arise more from the want of proper culture than from inherent wickedness."

"But, mamma," asked Ella, "was not their mock meeting very wicked — almost blasphemous?"

"Yes, it was very wicked," replied her mother, "but not so wicked for them as it would be for you."

"How can that be? Is not the same act as wicked in one person as another?"

"You have been taught from your infancy to respect religion and religious worship, and to speak the name of God reverently. They have had no such instruction; they have lived here, at the west, away from Sabbath schools and churches, and are alike ignorant of the divine precepts and penalties; and the Bible says, 'such shall be beaten with few stripes.' And now I will tell you how I think you may be benefited by occasional intercourse even with those whose moral characters are not what we could wish. You, my daughters, have thus far been brought in contact only with the refined and intelligent portion of the community; your morals have been carefully guarded, and your young minds kept from the influences of bad precept or example. While this course has had a happy effect in making you love all that is lovely, pure, and beautiful in mind as well as matter, it has led you into some false views of life, which you now have an opportunity to correct. You, Mary, are inclined to a fastidiousness, a morbid sensibility, which would rather bury itself in a cloister than come in contact with those whose virtuous characters and polished manners do not equal, or nearly so, your *beau ideal* of moral loveliness. You, Ella, are differently constituted. You become indignant, and are inclined to treat with contempt all those whom you find below your standard of morality; overlooking whatever is praiseworthy in their character or conduct. Now, my dear girls, I do not wish you to be on more than friendly terms with those whom you can not respect. I neither wish you to imitate their example nor copy their manners; but in this wilderness, shut out as we are from a choice of associates, and living, too, where there are no distinctions in society, we must not neglect the cultivation of the social principle implanted in our natures. Situated as we are, we must constantly strive to improve ourselves, and at the same time exercise patience and forbearance toward the failings of those around us, remembering that one of the best ways to prepare for future usefulness is to learn, while **young, to look** upon human life, not as it might be, but as it really is. We have talked a long while, and must now dismiss this subject for the present."

The next afternoon, when Mrs. Cleveland and her daughters had taken their sewing, Mary resumed the conversation of the previous day, by saying, " Ella and I found ourselves in quite a dilemma yesterday, mamma; and if you are not tired of answering questions, we would like to have you solve the problem for us."

" Your mother is never tired of answering questions, when her children feel disposed to profit by her instructions. So what was your dilemma, Mary?"

" Why, the girls asked us a great many questions about our domestic affairs; among the rest, if we allowed Mike and Kate to eat with us when we lived in the city. I told them no. And when they wanted to know the reason, I said I supposed it was because we had such a large family. Then they asked us if they ate the same food in the kitchen that we did in the dining room; if they ate with us every day now; if you thought your hired help as good as yourself; and so many more that I got tired, and told them they must excuse us from answering any more questions."

"Inquisitiveness is called a Yankee trait of character, and a most disagreeable one it is, too," remarked Mrs. Cleveland. "But, Mary, you did not give the true reason why Mike and Kate used to eat in the kitchen; for you recollect our table was large enough to afford room for more than our own family."

"I never thought any thing about it, and did not know what to say; but what was the true reason, mamma?"

"You have heard the old maxim, 'When you are in Rome, you must do as Romans do;' in other words, it was not customary there; and our faithful Katy would have felt quite out of her element to have been obliged to come in her kitchen dress, and sit down to her meals with the spruce young clerks; nor would Mike have been any more happy than she, to come in upon the carpet with his clothes soiled and shoes dusty. Then there were the chambermaid and errand boy; how embarrassed and awkward they would have appeared in such a position! All of them would have felt that a crust of bread and a glass of water by themselves were preferable to the most sumptuous repast under such circumstances. Their food was always the same as ours; and in giving them a separate table, we conferred a favor, rather than obliged them to submit to a degradation. Here the manners and customs are altogether different. All labor, all dress nearly alike, and the distinctions which there existed, and which were undoubtedly for the happiness of each class, are here unknown; and it would be both impolitic and ungenerous to attempt their introduction. As to thinking my domestics as good as myself, the Bible says, that 'God made of one blood all the nations of men that dwell on the face of the earth.' Besides, I am too much of a republican to believe in any other distinctions than those that naturally arise between the virtuous and vicious, the educated and uneducated, and those of different tastes and habits. These distinctions are not incompatible with Christianity; and being productive of the greatest amount of happiness to all concerned, can not be wrong. Is your problem solved, Mary?"

"Thank you, mamma, it is, satisfactorily. But, now, one more question. Mrs. Smith's daughters boasted a great deal about their father's riches, saying he was proprietor of the village, owning all except the few lots already built upon, had a number of farms, &c. Do you know whether Mr. Smith is wealthy or not?"

"I asked your father the same question, after I visited there," replied Mrs. Cleveland, "and he said that Mr. Smith came here seven or eight years ago, and located enough land in the vicinity for four or five good farms, any of which, near a market, would have been valuable. But here, though good land and well situated, they are much less so. A part of the one on which he lives he laid out in village lots; on the others he placed tenants. By tavern-keeping, petty speculating, &c., he has probably become worth five or six thousand dollars — quite a fortune here, and one which himself and family deem inexhaustible; but his neighbors begin to fear that his rum-drinking propensity, his wife's slatternly mode of housekeeping,—though she is a hard-working woman,—and the habits of idleness and ignorance in which they are training their children, will reduce them to poverty, if not to pauperism. You can see, my dear children, in the case of this family,—acknowledged by all to be the most wealthy in the vicinity,—how little of true respect the possession of wealth will command, unless accompanied by intelligence and moral worth."

CHAPTER VII.

SHALL WE HAVE A SABBATH SCHOOL?

<pre>
            Are there for feeble lambs
No shepherds? None to guide to living waters—
To break the bread of life to those that hunger,
Or pour the oil of joy into the stricken heart—
To touch the springs of feeling, and gently lead
The trembling penitent to Mercy's fount?
                            E. M. S.
</pre>

What can be done for the religious welfare of this community? was a question which often arose in the minds of Mr. and Mrs. Cleveland, especially on the Sabbath. Very seldom was there preaching of any kind, and when a minister of the gospel did visit the place, there was so much irreverence manifested by a large share of the audience, that no good effect seemed to be produced.

Yet these occasional Sabbath services were the means of bringing the people together for miles around, and the Clevelands were much gratified to find that a number of the families were refined, intelligent, and educated people, driven west by the same commercial misfortunes which had affected themselves; but alas! all were destitute of the pearl of great price — the only enduring riches.

In the village, Mr. and Mrs. Brown were the only professing Christians, and the two families soon became much attached to each other.

"We are alone," said Mr. Cleveland one day while conversing with Mr. Brown; "we are the only representatives of our Master; are we doing all we can for this perishing people?"

"I wish we might establish a Sabbath school. I can not think of any thing else that we could do," replied Mr. Brown.

"Mrs. Cleveland and I have often spoken of the same thing," said Mr. Cleveland; "suppose we make the attempt. Your wife would be a teacher; would she not?"

"Yes, gladly; she has longed for some work to do for Christ ever since we came here."

"And she has done good service in the quiet influence of a holy life," remarked Mr. Cleveland.

"Yes, you can not imagine what a blessing she has been to me; I fear I should have wandered far away but for her," said Mr. Brown, with much feeling. "Yet my wife says a Christian's duties extend beyond her own family circle, and I believe she is right."

"Certainly she is," replied Mr. Cleveland, "and it becomes us all to ask ourselves why Providence has placed us in this community, and to inquire of the Lord what he will have us to do. We may as well talk a little about that Sabbath school now as any time, if you are at leisure."

"Yes, I can spare an hour as well as not, and the sooner the work is commenced the better."

"It seems to me that all we have to do is to give out notice in the district school that a Sabbath school will be commenced next Sabbath," said Mr. Cleveland. "We will talk about the advantages of such a school with all we happen to meet during the week, then come together on the Sabbath, and organize the school with such materials as Providence may send. We shall meet with some opposition, I presume, but I do not apprehend any thing serious; do you?"

"There may be some difficulty in obtaining the use of the school house," replied Mr. Brown.

"You are one of the directors, are you not?" asked Mr. Cleveland, with surprise.

"Yes, but Mr. Smith and Mr. Johnson are the other two, and they are not very favorable to any religious movement," said Mr. Brown. "Besides, Mr. and Mrs. Smith are not pleased because Clara takes lessons with your children," he added, hesitatingly.

"Will it not be best for *me* to go and see

the other directors before we do any thing more?" asked Mr. Cleveland. "I suppose *you* are willing we should occupy the school house," he added, laughing.

"Yes, I believe so," replied Mr. Brown.

"I have a little leisure to-day," said Mr. Cleveland, "and will go and see them at once, and report to you on my return."

"Good morning, Mr. Smith; a very fine morning, sir," said Mr. Cleveland, stepping up to a railing in one corner of the bar room, behind which Mr. Smith was performing the duties of postmaster.

" Good morning, sir, good morning; glad you've come; here's two letters and a heap of papers for you," said Mr. Smith. " Guess if you should move out of town we should have to shut up the post office;" and he laughed uproariously at his attempt at witty compliment.

"Oh, not quite so bad as that," said Mr. Cleveland, smiling. "I have a little business with you as soon as you are at liberty," he added.

"I believe I am through now till some one else comes in," said Mr. Smith, turning around from the row of shelves filled with letters and papers, and leaning lazily against the railing.

"I came to inquire if you have any objection to the school house being occupied two hours every Sabbath by a Sabbath school?" asked Mr. Cleveland.

"I don't suppose the young ones would hurt the school house any, but seems to me five days and a half is quite as much time as children ought to be kept in school, and I should think the teacher would want to rest over Sunday, too," said Mr. Smith.

"Oh, you know a Sabbath school is expressly for studying the Bible, and any one who loves that holy book can be a teacher. I suppose you were accustomed to Sabbath schools when you lived at the east," said Mr. Cleveland.

"No; I have always lived in a new country — was born in the Genesee Valley when it was all woods, and came here as soon as the land was for sale; so, you see, I don't know much about religion, and all those new-fangled notions."

"I think you would like to have your children attend the Sabbath school," said Mr. Cleveland, "and you would look in upon us occasionally."

"Well, I don't know; I shouldn't like to give my consent to have the school house used unless I knew who would be the teachers, and what they would charge."

"I shall be one of the teachers, and Mrs. Cleveland another, and we hope a number of others will volunteer; perhaps you would be one," said Mr. Cleveland. "As for the price, we do not want any pay; it will be a great privilege to teach the dear children the way to heaven."

"I guess I wouldn't do for a teacher, then," remarked Mr. Smith, "for I don't know the way myself; but, as you say, I would like to have my children learn; so you may have the school house, for what I care. I suppose you've got Brown's consent; he's a wonderful pious man, you know."

"Yes, and I hope he will be one of the teachers; you consider him a Christian, do you not?" asked Mr. Cleveland, a little anxiously.

"Oh, yes, I guess so; though I never could understand how he should be so quiet and *submissive*, I believe you call it, when little Annie died; I should have raved like a madman. She was the sweetest little thing I ever saw; they hadn't been here more than three months when she died."

"That is just what religion is good for," said Mr. Cleveland; "it helps us to bear every affliction patiently, knowing that ' our Father doeth all things well.' "

"I don't know any thing about it, but you can have the school house," said Mr. Smith.

"Good morning, Mr. Simpson; glad to see you." And Mr. Smith went behind the bar to wait on a rum customer with the air of a man glad to be released from an unpleasant position.

"I think I will go right down and see Mr. Johnson," said Mr. Cleveland. "Good morning."

"Good morning, sir, good morning," replied Mr. Smith, rubbing his hands and nodding.

Mr. Johnson's farm was a mile from the village, and the sun was becoming uncomfortably warm,— for it was now ten o'clock in the morning of a sultry day in July,— and Mr. Cleveland felt the depressing effect both of the weather and the interview. "Desolation, desolation!" he exclaimed, as he turned away from the door of that miserable tavern; "to think of bringing up my children amid such influences!" and for a moment the earthly father's heart rebelled against that heavenly Father whose providence had placed them there. 'Twas but for a moment. "Oh, forgive me, for I have sinned, and help me to say, 'Even so, Father, for so it seemeth good in thy sight,'" was the sweet outbreathing of an obedient spirit; and all again was peace.

Most of the way lay through a dense forest, with only a wagon track marked out by blazed trees, and the cool shade of the thick canopy of green above him was very grateful. The morning song of the birds had ceased, but they flitted hither and thither among the green boughs, and he heard now and then a loving twitter over some late nest of fledglings. Nimble squirrels ran up the trunks of the trees, or chattered saucily from the overhanging boughs, and the timid rabbit leaped nervously away from the approaching footsteps. All nature was in the maturity of its summer glory, and Mr. Cleveland soon found his own spirit attuned to the harmony of nature. "O Lord, I will not distrust thee," he exclaimed; "hast thou not said, 'The wilderness and the solitary place shall be glad for them, and the desert shall rejoice and blossom as the rose?' Surely, I came here because thou hast a work for me to do; give me grace to do thy holy will."

Mr. Johnson's house and farm had an

appearance of greater thrift and comfort than Mr. Cleveland had expected; the fences were in good repair, and he noticed with peculiar pleasure that shade trees had been left standing; in the front yard and along the path to the gate were well-kept beds of flowers. Near the house, on the right, a small orchard waved its young boughs cheerily, and on the left a field of wheat, almost ready for the harvest, nodded in golden glory. Further in the distance, fields of corn and potatoes looked green and promising. Opening the rude gate, he slowly approached the house, vainly scanning the fields, to discover their owner. All was still; the children, he knew, were at school, and doubtless Mrs. Johnson was busy with her domestic affairs. He reached the house, and rapped on the open door.

"Come in," said a feeble voice.

Mr. Cleveland entered, and was surprised to see Mr. Johnson attempting to rise from a bed which stood in one corner of the room.

"Oh, good morning, Mr. Cleveland," said he; "I am glad to see you; walk in, and help yourself to a chair."

"Why, I am surprised to find you sick," exclaimed Mr. Cleveland, stepping forward and shaking hands with the sick man.

"Only the ague, I think," said Mr. Johnson, "but it affects me worse than it ever did before; I have been sick only a few days, yet I am very weak;" and he sank back on his pillow.

"Only the ague!" repeated Mr. Cleveland; "what would you have worse? I think it one of the worst diseases I ever saw, though I never suffered from it."

"Yes, it is bad enough, but you know it don't kill people; so a man never gets pitied if he has it ever so hard."

"The rest of your family are all well, I hope."

"Yes, quite well, I thank you."

Mrs. Johnson now came in, and was introduced to Mr. Cleveland. Her manners were quiet and pleasing, very unlike those of Mrs. Smith, with whom Mr. Cleveland had unconsciously associated her. After a few minutes spent in conversation, Mrs. Johnson withdrew to attend to her household duties.

"I have called on two of the directors to get their permission to open a Sabbath school in the school house, and came to get your consent also," said Mr. Cleveland.

"I shall be very glad to have a Sabbath school established; my poor children are growing up like the heathen," said Mr. Johnson, with emotion.

"Will you not help us in the good work when you get well?" asked Mr. Cleveland.

"I — I help you? Why, Mr. Cleveland, don't you know I am a wicked man? I don't know the way myself; how then can I teach others?"

"First learn the way yourself. Do you not feel the need of an all-sympathizing Friend, now in your illness?" asked Mr. Cleveland.

"Yes, indeed," replied Mr. Johnson; "the subject has scarcely been out of my mind since I called at your house that first Sabbath after you came, and I have not patronized Mr. Smith's tavern since. I have longed to come and tell you my feelings, but could not muster the courage. I want to become a Christian, but do not quite understand what I am to do."

"The gospel plan is so simple that we can scarcely believe it," remarked Mr. Cleveland. "Repentance toward God, and faith in our Lord Jesus Christ, are the only conditions of our pardon and acceptance with him."

"I know it all seems very simple, but after all I can't quite understand it," said Mr. Johnson, with a sigh.

"Perhaps I can help you some," said Mr. Cleveland, tenderly, for he knew how thick seems the spiritual darkness when the soul first begins to feel its necessities. "Repent; be sorry, really sorry that you have sinned, and resolve, with God's help, to forsake all your sinful course, and live a life of obedience to the precepts of the gospel. Believe that Jesus died to save you, not only from the penalty of God's broken law, but from your own sinful self, and that he is willing and waiting to adopt you into his family, and finally to give you a crown of glory in heaven."

"But must not I pray a great deal, and read the Bible, and do all I can to make myself better, before I believe?" asked Mr. Johnson.

"No; you must believe now, at once; give yourself right up to him, sins and all, just as you are, and let Christ forgive you and save you. You can not make yourself any better — you do not feel that you are any better than you were when you first began to think of this subject; do you? And yet I presume you have read the Bible, and prayed a great deal; have you not?"

"Yes, I have read, and prayed, and thought, till I have been almost discouraged, for I seem to be growing worse and worse, more and more wicked every day," said Mr. Johnson, with a sigh.

"Then you feel more and more the need of one who will redeem you from all this sin and wretchedness," said Mr. Cleveland. "Jesus came to save *sinners* — not the righteous. Can you not give yourself up to him to be saved in his own way?"

"I will try. Will you pray with me, Mr. Cleveland?" asked Mr. Johnson, in an imploring tone.

"Gladly," was the reply; and Mr. Cleveland knelt by the sick man's bedside, and poured out his soul in prayer for the conversion of the soul, and for the speedy recovery of the bodily health.

"Amen!" was the heartfelt response of the sick man, when the prayer was ended.

"I have made you a long visit," said Mr. Cleveland, after a few minutes' conversation; "let me beg you to adopt the language of these beautiful lines as your own resolve: —

> 'Just as I am, without one plea
> But that thy blood was shed for me,
> And that thou bidd'st me come to thee,
> O Lamb of God, I come!'"

> 'Just as I am, and waiting not
> To rid my soul from one dark blot,
> To thee, whose blood can cleanse each spot,
> O Lamb of God, I come!'"

"I am so thankful you came!" said Mr. Johnson, grasping Mr. Cleveland's hand: "a kind Providence sent you, I am sure."

"Not a sparrow falls to the ground without his notice; and will he not direct *us*, if we only submit ourselves to his guidance?" said Mr. Cleveland. "Give yourself entirely into his hands; trust him fully; 'only believe.'"

With a light step, and a heart full of prayer and praise, did Mr. Cleveland wend his way homeward. He had caught a glimpse of the loving Father's purpose in bringing him hither. Oh, if he might be the means of leading souls to Jesus! With tearful eyes he related to Mr. Brown the success of his interviews, and with warmly-clasped hands, they mutually pledged themselves to prayer and unwearied effort for the salvation of the community in which God had placed them.

CHAPTER VIII.

THE SABBATH SCHOOL BEGUN.

> See those who are by grace made free
> Bend o'er each class with soul-lit eye,
> Point to the Lamb of Calvary,
> And speak of hopes which cannot die;
> While answering look and heaving breast
> Assert the truth received with zest.
> E. M. S.

The news that there was to be a Sabbath school organized the next Sabbath had been most industriously circulated by the children, and variously discussed by their elders, during the week; and when Saturday night came, many bright eyes were scanning the sky for weather-signs for the morrow.

Sunday morning dawned at last, bright and beautiful. As there was to be no preaching, the Sabbath school meeting had been appointed at the usual hour of morning service. Long before the time, parents, with children of all ages, from overgrown school girls, and great, awkward boys, to "toddling wee things," — for it had gone forth that there would be an infant class, — were seen emerging from the forest in every direction; and when the Cleveland family arrived, prompt to the hour, they found the rather capacious log school house well filled.

Mr. Brown rose, and stated the object for which they were assembled, and called on Mr. Cleveland to conduct the exercises as he thought proper.

Mr. Cleveland took a Bible from his pocket, and read the Saviour's invitation to little children. He then asked the children if any of them could sing "Happy Land." Half a dozen little hands were raised, and with the aid of a few Sabbath school hymn books, the song which every child loves was very well sung. In simple and appropriate language, Mr. Cleveland then besought the divine blessing on this attempt to serve Him, and most fervently did he implore the descent of the Holy Spirit, with its reviving influences and converting power. He then gave a brief history of the rise, progress, and design of Sabbath schools, and closed by asking the question, "Shall we to-day organize a Sabbath school, and will we mutually agree to help sustain it and give it interest?" Calling for free remarks from all present, he then took his seat.

A few expressed their gratification that their children would again enjoy the privilege of religious instruction, and a total silence ensued.

Close by the door sat Mr. Smith. At length he arose, and, wiping his forehead with a large red bandana, said he had no objections to the school, if it would pay its own way. "For my part," said he, "I think the day school is enough; and I am sure the school taxes are high enough.

I know the teachers are not paid, and we give the use of the school house; but there must be some expense somewhere. Now I should like to know just what it is, before I vote for the school."

"I am very glad you mentioned the subject," said Mr. Cleveland; "and I should be happy to tell you beforehand all I know of the matter. To have a first-rate school, we shall need a Sabbath school library, costing seven or ten dollars, and Testaments and singing books, costing about seven more; then every year we shall need about five dollars' worth of new books, to keep up the interest of the children. If we continue the school during the winter, it will take one or two loads of wood. I do not know of any other expense."

"Well, I should think that was enough. Fourteen dollars, at least, to begin with. I wonder who has that amount of money to give! I'm sure I have not;" and, seizing his hat, he pushed it down over his eyes, and walked out.

"The difficulty of raising money is obviated for the present, at least," said Mr.

Cleveland, addressing the audience. "The Sabbath school with which I was connected in New York gave me a complete library, to be used in the village where I should reside; and I hope by next year we shall love the Sabbath school so well, that its necessary expenses will seem rather a pleasure than a burden. The children are getting restless. Shall we try that same song again, children?"

There was a fine show of little hands, and "Happy Land" was sung with greatly increased zest.

"Shall we now take a vote on the organization of the school?" asked Mr. Cleveland. A motion was made by Mr. Brown, that a Sabbath school be organized and sustained. The motion was supported by Mr. Dascomb, a new settler, who lived about two miles distant, and the affirmative vote was unanimous. Mr. Cleveland was then elected superintendent, Mr. Brown assistant, and Mr. Dascomb librarian.

Mr. Cleveland briefly thanked his neighbors for the honor conferred, and pledged himself, by divine assistance, to be faithful to the spiritual interests of their children.

With Mr. Brown's assistance, he then proceeded to classify the scholars. This portion of the work was soon accomplished. Teachers were provided as far as they could be obtained; Mrs. Cleveland being duly installed over the infant class, whose long, low seat was placed across the capacious fireplace; and more than one little face was upturned to catch a glimpse of the blue sky through the broad top of the stick chimney.

The lesson for the next Sabbath was given out, and the teachers spent a little time in hearing their classes read, making such changes in the first arrangement as seemed necessary, and explaining the lesson as an assistance to the undisciplined minds of the little ones. Mrs. Cleveland chatted pleasantly with her little flock, and completely won their hearts by telling of the dear Saviour's love for little children.

The school was then closed by singing a doxology, and the assembly quietly dispersed.

"Now, if we could only have a prayer meeting, to ask the blessing of God upon these efforts, I should feel that we were really getting into something like working order," said Mr. Cleveland, as he and Mr. Brown were slowly walking homeward.

"I wish your family would come to my house at five o'clock this evening," said Mr. Brown; "we might have a meeting large enough to claim the promise."

"Thank you; we will if Mrs. Cleveland is not too much fatigued. I was quite surprised to meet with so little opposition to-day. Didn't you expect more?"

"Yes; but the greatest trial-time has not yet come," was the reply. "When the novelty wears off, there will probably be a reaction."

"Unless, by the blessing of God, some of these hearts should become enlisted in his service. Oh, let us pray earnestly for this," said Mr. Cleveland, with emotion.

"We will!" was the earnest response; and these two laborers, to whom God had given this great field of missionary effort, sought each his home and his closet.

CHAPTER IX.

THE PRAYER MEETING.

Still on beyond time's utmost bounds
  Around the throne of God in heaven
Their reunited praise resounds
  For grace received and sins forgiven ;
And 'mong the gifts of priceless worth
Was named the Sabbath school on earth.
E. M. S.

"MOTHER, mother! I guess we can have a Sabbath school, if we do live in the woods," said little Lottie Dascomb, clapping her hands joyfully, as she ran into the house.

"Gently, gently, my child you will wake the baby," said her mother, smiling at the child's enthusiasm. "Put away your bonnet, my dear, and then come and tell me all about the new school." The delighted child skipped away, and the mother was soon listening to a minute account of the whole meeting. "And father was chosen librarian. What is a librarian, mother?" asked Lottie, with a puzzled look.

"A librarian is one who takes care of the

books, and gives them out to the children," replied her mother.

"But he does not give them to us to keep; does he, mother?"

"No; he numbers them all; then, when you take one, he writes down the number opposite your name, and when you bring that one back he crosses off that number, and puts down the number of the new book which you take. Do you understand it?"

"Oh, yes," said Lottie. "I am so glad we have a Sabbath school! I guess I shall not grow up a heathen, if I do live at the west. Cousin Lucy said I would."

"I hope not," replied her mother, smiling.

Mr. Cleveland's children were almost as enthusiastic as little Lottie, and their tongues ran merrily for a time.

"Mamma, I think you had more than your share of scholars to-day," said Ella; "and they were not all quite of an age, either."

"Not very much difference in age, I think," said Mrs. Cleveland; "and you know the infant class should be large. I thought there were quite too few."

"Ella refers to that long seat full of

young men, who sat right behind you, and would not join any class," said Mary.

"They were very attentive listeners," remarked Mr. Cleveland; "and if they will come even to hear what you and others say, it may do them good."

"Certainly," said Mrs. Cleveland; "but I should have been embarrassed if I had known they were there. However, I will try to be prepared for it now. Having the children sit in the fireplace is a nice arrangement for me," she added; "I am not compelled to face the audience."

"But it is so funny to see the children looking up the chimney!" said Ella.

"Mr. Brown invited us to come to his house this afternoon for a little prayer meeting. Shall we go?" said Mr. Cleveland, addressing his wife.

"Oh, yes; I should like it very much," was her reply, in a glad tone.

"May we go, too, papa?" asked Mary.

"Yes, as many of you as wish," said her father.

That afternoon a prayer meeting was established in Smithton.

"O father, father! I wish you and mother had been at the Sabbath school to-day, we had such a nice time," said Fannie Johnson, a child five years old, as she threw her weary little self into a chair, and leaned her head down on the side of the bed.

Mr. Johnson passed his hand caressingly over the little head wet with perspiration. "Did you have a pleasant time, too, Lizzie?" said he, addressing his oldest daughter.

"Yes, father; and I hope you and mother will both be able to go next Sabbath. I think you will like it."

"Who is your teacher, little puss?" asked the father, patting Fannie's head.

"Mrs. Cleveland," replied the child; "and, O father," she exclaimed, starting up, "she told us such a pretty story about Jesus! She said he loved little children, and even wicked men and women, so well, that he came clear down from heaven to die for them, so that they could go to heaven and live with him for ever. And now, she said, any body who would only love the dear Saviour, would certainly go to heaven; children, too! just think of it! Did you know that, father?"

"Yes, my child; I was told that when I was a very little boy."

"But you never told me, father."

"No, my child, and I am very sorry."

"Do you love that dear Jesus, father?"

"I hope I do, my daughter," said Mr. Johnson, with emotion. "I have only just begun to love him, and I want so much to get well, and then we can all read the Bible and pray together, morning and night. Would you like that, Fannie?"

"Yes, indeed! and I guess mother would like it, too. Wouldn't you, mother?"

"Certainly, I should have no objections," replied Mrs. Johnson, coldly. Rising immediately, she passed into the kitchen to prepare a lunch for the tired children.

Poor Mr. Johnson! This was the first time he had dared to confess his love for the Saviour. It had been a great cross; and now, she, who, of all others, he thought would rejoice most, had chilled him to the soul. Why was this? She was a professing Christian when he married her. Had she learned the fallacy of her own hopes, and so felt saddened that he had fallen into the same snare? His nerves were weakened by sickness, and this sudden reaction was too much; the tears rolled down his cheeks, and his breast heaved with emotion.

"Don't cry, father;" whispered little Fannie, wiping away his tears with her apron. "It isn't wrong to love Jesus. I wish I loved him, too. Will he really help me to love him, if I ask him, as Mrs. Cleveland said?"

"Yes, darling. Now run away a little while, and let father think."

"And pray in your heart, too, I guess." And the little one kissed him, and quietly slid down, and ran out into the yard.

Mrs. Johnson's mind was in a perfect tumult. Her husband converted while she had been a wanderer; scarcely praying, even in form, either for him or for herself. He was a Christian. Was she one? Dared she hope, when she had so sadly neglected a wife's holiest duty? She could not weep; she dared not pray; and, calling her children to their lunch, she was just passing out of the door to get away from human sight for a time, when she heard her husband calling her.

"I think Mr. Cleveland's visit was greatly blessed to me. Will you forgive me for not telling you sooner?" said Mr. Johnson, as his wife approached the bed-side. "You are glad I love the Saviour; are you not?"

"Yes. But, O James, I need to ask your forgiveness and the forgiveness of my Father in heaven," exclaimed Mrs. Johnson, bursting into tears; "I have been so unfaithful as a professedly Christian wife and mother."

"You had no one to help you along, dear wife, and it is very hard for a loving woman to go on alone; rather a dangerous experiment to marry an irreligious man, as you did; but I will try to help you now; and He who has so freely pardoned me will also forgive you, and bless us both in his service, I trust."

The children now came running in; and, with a significant look, Mrs. Johnson rose and left the room.

When she returned, an hour later, her face bespoke that peace which the world can not give, and the last rays of the Sabbath sun rested on no happier earthly abode than that rude forest home.

CHAPTER X.

FRUITS.

Still on it creeps,
Each little moment at another's heels,
Till hours, days, years, and ages are made up
Of such small parts as these, and men look back
Worn and bewildered, wondering how it is.
     JOANNA BAILLIE'S RAYNER.

WE will pass over an interval of ten years, equal in the growth of western cities and villages to a century of olden time.

Smithton is now a large, populous town, with no other marks of its identity than are to be found in the older, yet familiar faces of its early inhabitants.

The clatter of machinery, the hum of many mills, the thronging teams, and the ringing tread of rapid footsteps assure you of its business prosperity; while that large, well-built Union school house, and those four commodious churches, show that the mental and moral wants of the community are by no means overlooked.

Our old friends are all here — all, save the proprietor of the village, poor Mr. Smith. For a few years he annoyed by his petty persecutions those who sought to promote the best interests of himself and his children, his course constantly tending more and more rapidly downward, till at last he sank, past recovery, into the pit he had digged for the unwary; a few days he raved in wild delirium, and passed into a hopeless eternity, another victim to *rum*. His children grew up miserable spendthrifts, and all that paternal inheritance, which seemed so inexhaustible, now has other ownership, and they are thriftless leeches on an industrious community.

That first Sabbath school passed successfully through the trials and vicissitudes of the first winter, and has never for one Sabbath been omitted. And that little prayer meeting in Mr. Brown's parlor became the birthplace of many precious souls. They assemble in the church now, and Mr. Johnson's voice is often heard in prayer and exhortation. Lottie Dascom's father is one of the deacons, and she has consecrated her young, beautiful life to the service of her Redeemer.

Our first friends, the Clevelands, are prosperous and happy; all their children are gathered into the visible church, and rejoicingly the parents are laboring on in the service of Him who has signally proved himself a covenant-keeping God.

The broad and beautiful west, with all its moral desolations, is the subject of much prayerful thought to their oldest son, George, and the parents fondly hope he may be a chosen laborer in this part of the Saviour's promised inheritance. For here, as every where,—

> "The harvest dawn is near,
>   The year delays not long,
> And he who sows with many a tear
>   Shall reap with many a song.
>
> "Sad to his toil he goes,
>   His seed with weeping leaves;
> But he shall come at twilight's close,
>   And bring his golden sheaves."

www.ingramcontent.com/pod-product-compliance
Lightning Source LLC
Chambersburg PA
CBHW020301090426
42735CB00009B/1176